if you give your teacher a cookie,

She's going to want a drink to go with it.

All the sugar will give her
lots of energy.
She'll want to go shopping!

While she's doing her shopping, she'll find some really cute pens

She'll then want to go home and make some crafts!

All the crafting will make her tired. She'll want to get comfy!

Once she's nice and comfy, she'll want something to eat.

And chances are, if she has something to eat, she'll want a cookie to go with it!

love,

best memory

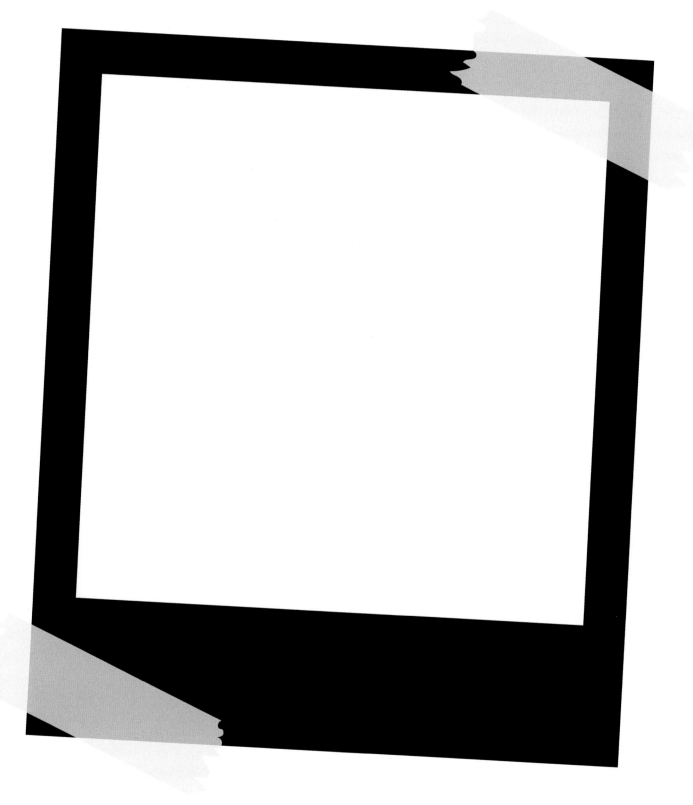

best memory

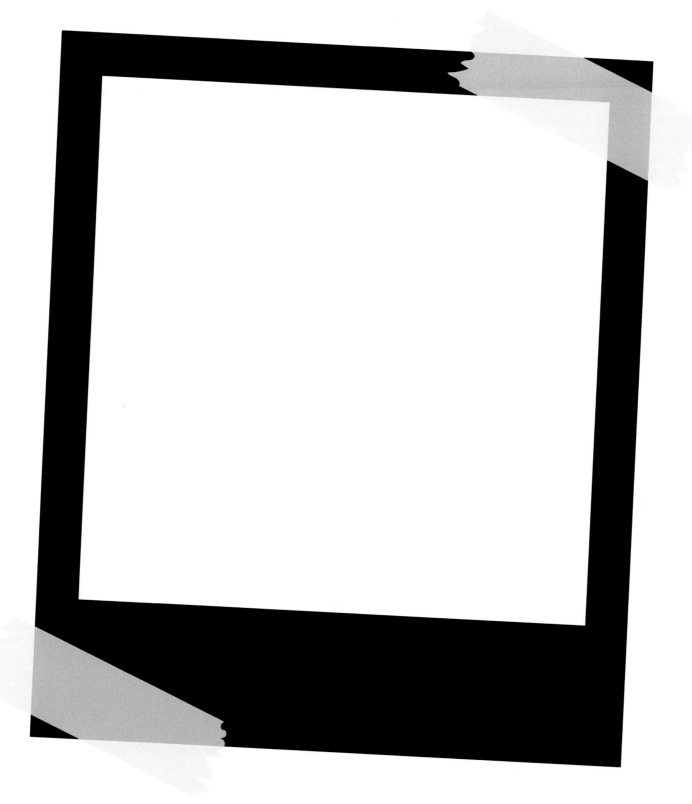

YOU'RE MY **FAVORITE**

TEACHER ♥

Made in the USA
Las Vegas, NV
10 December 2024

13792016R00017